CW00971512

How to Let Your Holiday Home

As a Profitable Business

Content Copyright © Dori Joyner

June 2013

All Rights Reserved

Table of Contents

Introduction

So you have a holiday home. All you have to do now is furnish it, equip it, fill it with lovely people, all summer long, who will treasure your possessions, leave your home immaculately clean, re-book for next year and you will be laughing all the way to the bank. If only it were that simple!

It doesn't matter if your holiday home is a villa in Florida, a chalet in the Swiss Alps or an apartment on the Black Sea, the principle is the same. We all want the same thing; lots of holiday weeks booked in our property year after year.

- But how do you get this business up and running? And once it is, how do you make sure you make as much profit as possible?

- How are you planning on marketing it? Will you have a website? A brochure?

- Where will you advertise it? How much can you spend on marketing?

- Will you accept children or animals? Is your property child friendly?

- Is the property suitable for the disabled?

- How many weeks do you hope to rent out the property?

- Will you want to use the property as a holiday home for yourself?

- Are you prepared to offer short breaks?

- Could you offer special interest holidays, such as fishing, wine tasting, cycling or horse riding?

- How much are you thinking of charging? What are other local holiday home owners charging?

- What will your charges include? Electricity, water, perhaps firewood?

- How are you going to collect your rent? Will you take credit cards or use PayPal?

- How are you going to furnish and equip your holiday home?

- Will you supply bed linen and towels? If so how will you launder them? Is there a commercial laundry nearby?

- What facilities are available at the property? Satellite TV? Internet access?

- Will you have a pool? How long will it take to recoup the cost of installing a pool?

- Do you live near your holiday home? If not, who will meet and greet your guests? Who will be there on change over day to see guests off, clean the house, make up the beds and welcome the next lot of visitors?

- Will you rely on neighbours to help out or will you employ a property management company?

- What about emergencies? Is there a doctor or hospital nearby? Or maybe a plumber?

- What about the tax situation? Will you need an accountant?

- What about insurance? Do you have Public Liability insurance?

I have probably raised questions here you haven't thought of, but, trust me, there will be more.

We have had two holiday homes in France for 12 years and it is pretty fair to say that we were far too naive at the beginning, but we have learnt from our mistakes over the years. Today we also run a French Property Management business for owners who want to rent out their property as a holiday home. Sometimes, when talking to new prospective holiday home owners, we forget that it has taken us all this time to become experts in the field. That is why I decided to put our experiences to good use and write this book.

During the last decade we have made many new friends and only a few I would rather not welcome to my homes again!

It's not an easy job, but it once you have all the systems in place it should all go like clockwork.

So, in this book I have tried to explain how to make the most of your holiday home in sensible step-by-step chapters.

Owning a holiday home can be such a rewarding business, enjoy!

Hirondelle Farm

I thought it would be a good idea to tell you how I became such an authority on holiday homes, by explaining how we came to be holiday home owners!

I moved to France with my husband, Dave, and three cats back in 2001. We bought a farmhouse and 4 barns, which had been derelict for almost 40 years. It cost us less than we had paid for our first 3 bedroomed semi on the south coast of England back in the 1970's.

In August 2000 we were in France looking for a two-up-two-down holiday home just for ourselves. We had no intention, at that time, of giving up our jobs, selling our home, moving abroad and venturing into the tourist world by becoming proprietors of holiday homes.

We were heading towards the Dordogne in search of the sun, where we had been informed, (wrongly) shone only south of the Loire. I remember feeling a bit feverish waiting for the ferry to leave Portsmouth, but it was a very hot day. By the time we were driving through the Loire Atlantique the next day I felt really ill, so we stopped to look for a doctor. It transpired I was dehydrated, the doctor suggested we stayed in a local hotel for a couple of days before continuing on our journey.

So we found ourselves in a motel just outside Chateaubriant.

After a day or so resting we wandered into town on the Monday morning. Most of the shops were closed, as is the norm here. It allows people who work on a Saturday to still have a two day week-end. We stumbled upon what appeared to be the only estate agent who had opened up their office that day.

Although this was not the area we intended to invest in, we had nothing better to do that day. So we told him what we were looking for and explained we had a very tight budget. He showed us details of two properties, one was bang on budget the other was a bit over, but the agent assured us that the owner would come down in price.

So we set off in the agent's wife's car, an old Renault 4. He apologised for the toys scattered on the rear seat and told us his "proper" car was in the garage.

We didn't like the first place he showed us at all, there was another house at a strange angle almost across the front door, very odd. So we wound our way through narrow French lanes, hot on the bumper of any car which happened to be in front of us, until we came to a stop outside what eventually became the FarmHouse in Hirondelle Farm.

The agent's details had shown a house which looked like it might be suitable for our plans and as we looked around we realised that there was, indeed, some potential to turn this into our holiday home.

It was in quite a bad way, having been empty for such a long time. At that time there were only two downstairs rooms, the upper floor being used for grain storage and commonly called the hay loft. Access to the loft was via a ladder placed on the outside of the building and through the hay loft window, there was no staircase. The previous owner had lived there with no water, no electricity, no sewage, on beaten earth floors and shared the downstairs two rooms with a flock of geese.

The mind boggles.

The windows, and any remaining glass, were hidden from view by some old shutters barely hanging on their hinges. There were ferns growing in the fireplace, plaster was falling from the walls and the roof was on it's last legs. In short it was almost a ruin.

The ground floor measured about 10 metres by 6 metres. We thought that we could probably develop this into a good sized three bedroomed house, assuming we used the upstairs floor too.

As we emerged from the farmhouse the agent pointed opposite to a lovely stone built barn, which we later discovered, had been the stable, and said "That too". The stable turned out to be just a stone shell. On the ground floor there were some remains of what had been animal pens built on a beaten earth, and what we thought, was a cobblestoned floor. The upper floor was the same as the farmhouse in that it had only been used as storage, again there was no staircase. The roof of the stable was no better than the farmhouse but there was something very sweet about this building. It measured 9 metres by 5 metres, slightly smaller, but we thought we could transform this into a pretty two bedroomed house.

Then we walked around the corner to see 3 more barns on a huge plot of south facing land. The agent pointed to each in turn, "That too, that too, that too". The barns were adjacent to each other, but not interconnecting. Two large barns, in that they had hay lofts and therefore could have 2 floors, and a single storey barn sandwiched in between and set a little way back, so that a courtyard was formed and enclosed on two sides by the larger barns.

The taller barns measured 8 metres by 5 metres each and the single storey barn was 9 meters by 5 metres. The agent went to great lengths to explain that one was a hay barn, the middle smaller barn was the pig sty and at the opposite end was the cow shed. They were all in a worse state than the farmhouse and the stable. At the bottom of the garden there was a field of corn as high as an elephants eye. Talk about wow factor!

Just as we were getting over the shock of the size of this property, the agent remembered another bit of land he had forgotten to show us. This ran behind the farmhouse, the full width of the building and that of next door's. At some stage it had been an orchard, but that day, amid the waist high weeds, we could only find two pear trees.

The owner did indeed come down, a bit more than he expected to, thanks to Dave's negotiating skills!

We went back to the UK and wondered what we were going to do with our new French estate, it was not exactly what we had intended to buy. Eventually we decided that we could turn the original farmhouse and the stable into two holiday homes, then we could transform the remaining 3 barns into a house for ourselves,

We both have experience of renovating although we had never attempted anything quite so huge or quite so dilapidated. In all, we had 415 square metres of property to completely renovate, or in old money 4,467 square feet.

We arrived in February and parked our caravan in the courtyard in front of the pig sty, attached the awning and set up our temporary home. We lived in it for eight months.

As soon as the stable was barely liveable we moved in there, the caravan being far too hot to live in during the warmer months. I remember our TV, which was in the caravan awning, melted in the heat!

It took us just over a year of blood sweat and tears to transform the Stable into a beautiful 2 bedroomed home.

We kept the ground floor open plan, there's plenty of room for the lounge, fitted kitchen and our old pine dining table and chairs.

Our first guests arrived for their holiday in June 2002 by which time we had begun work on the farmhouse and moved back to into the caravan.

The farmhouse took longer to renovate, in fact longer than we though it would. About three weeks before our first guests there were due to arrive it suddenly hit us that we might not be finished. So we worked those last few weeks, night and day, seven days a week in a panic. I was still painting the garden gate when our visitors arrived.

Those first three years we moved every six weeks. We would live in which either of the holiday homes was empty at the time. If both were booked, back to the caravan we went.

So it was with much excitement that we planned for Dave to begin work on our house, which was to be the three adjacent barns in the south facing garden overlooking the corn field.

He began work on a cold, November, Tuesday morning about 8.00am, it must have been about two hours later when he fell through the upstairs floor and broke two ribs. So for the next six weeks Dave lay on the fold down sofa in the FarmHouse whilst I tried to find him things to do which needed very little effort.

So it was not until the beginning of 2005 that work finally began on our house, we moved in during March although we only had one room upstairs which was habitable. Nonetheless, it was ours, we didn't have to move back into the caravan ever again.

I wanted to put a match to the caravan by this time and even offered to dance around the blazing thing naked, but Dave decided it would make good storage. So today, it still stands in our garden. To be honest I don't think it would move if we wanted it to.

We have often been asked how much we spent transforming Hirondelle Farm, but we find it almost impossible to calculate. We did all the work ourselves so there were no labour costs. We bought all the materials when they were on special offer whether we needed them at the time or not. And of course we had the usual expenses of just living for the duration of the renovations.

There is a rule of thumb which says: 150 Euros per square metre for a general spruce up, 500 euros per square metre for a major overhaul, and 750 Euros per square metres for a new build or a re-build from a ruin.

If we base the renovations of the Stable on a re-build, the above would indicate that costs were 750 Euros a square metre which would mean that the Stable cost us 67,500 Euros to renovate. Had we employed a builder that figure might be just about right. But as we did all the work we would have spent much, much, less than that.

Of course, you should bear in mind that it's always going to be easier to spend more than to spend less.

Please note that figures quoted here are based on prices at the time of our renovations.

Furnishing Your Holiday Home

Guests demand more for their money nowadays and expect high standards in properties they rent for their holiday. If they wanted to sleep in a room that looks like a hotel bedroom they would have booked into a hotel. But they chose to rent a holiday home, the emphasis being on the word "home". So it must be furnished and equipped accordingly. This is certainly one business where you will get out what you put in. Consider every expense you incur in furnishing your holiday home as an investment in your business.

Of course you will want to have lovely furniture in your holiday home, but you will need practical furniture. There is little point in buying a sofa with cream linen nonremovable covers. No matter how great your guests are, they are not going to worry too much about the odd bit of chocolate or red wine getting on your sofa. On the other hand, don't expect your guest to re-book for another year if they have had to spend a week sitting on a tatty, uncomfortable sofa.

Don't buy too trendy either. The latest fashions soon go out of style and will look dated very soon, stick to the more traditional styles wherever possible. Leather is a good bet for sofas, easy to clean and hard wearing. But if you feel that leather can be too cold in the winter and hot and sticky in the summer, you could always add a (machine washable) throw over a leather sofa.

If you do buy a fabric covered sofa make sure the covers are removable and machine washable. Choose middle of the range colours, nothing to light or too dark. If possible buy two lots of sofa covers in case of accidents.

A good sized TV which is viewable from the far end of the room is a must. You should also provide home entertainments systems such as a music centre and DVD or Blu Ray player, plus a selection of music CDs and DVDs. Satellite TV is essential, as is an iPod docking station, a games system, some good board games and some paperback books. Don't forget the children who may stay in your property, have something that your smaller guests can play with.

Internet access is expected today and some visitors will actually base their search for a holiday home on whether or not it has Wi-Fi.

You should furnish your property towards minimalists trends rather than filling it with unnecessary furniture and ornaments. Don't be tempted to put in those two old dining chairs that you have no room for in your main home. A property furnished with mis-matched bits and pieces just smacks of lack of attention. Try to imagine that your holiday home is a stage set and all the furniture are stage props. Everything in your property is required for use during your guests' stays, everything has it's own place. If you think that something is surplus to requirements, take it out.

Don't try to squeeze in an extra bed on a landing and call it a mezzanine, just because you think you can charge more for a property which accommodates 7 people rather than 6. Think about where you would like to sleep.

Buy good quality beds, mattresses, pillows and bedding. Use protectors on the mattresses and pillows and leave extra pillows for your guests, in a suitable position in the property.

Plan to have one lot of bedding in use, one in the laundry basket and at the very least one in the linen cupboard at any given moment. The same applies to towels, supply one bath towel and one hand towel for each guest. Talking of which, buy the best you can afford. They do get such a lot of use and no one wants to step out from a lovely hot shower to dry themselves on a see-through limp bit of cotton.

Ensure that there is a sufficient supply of good clothes hangers in all the wardrobes. A hairdryer and a box of tissues are a nice touch on the dressing table, making sure that a suitable electric socket is nearby. A full length mirror is required too.

Keep in mind the number of guests your property accommodates. At the risk of stating the obvious, if you have three double bedrooms the chances are you will need enough sofas to accommodate six people and 6 dining chairs around a good sized dining table.

Remember, too that an under worktop fridge is fine for a family of 3 or four, but you will need a bigger fridge/freezer if your property can accommodate more visitors.

Don't assume that your guests will always eat out just because they are on holiday, a well equipped kitchen is a must. Imagine that it is your own kitchen. Buy two dinner services of the same design, but only put one in the house. Then, when a plate is broken replace it with one from the second set. This way 2 services last much longer. Apply the same logic to wine glasses.

A range of good saucepans with lids and a wok or deep frying pan are all necessary. As are a good set of knives and a chopping board - which should be clearly visible in the kitchen rather than hidden in a cupboard so that your guests don't find it until your worktops are damaged beyond repair! Tea towels, kitchen roll and basic stocks of tea, coffee, sugar should all be available. A bottle of local wine in the fridge would be appreciated I'm sure!

If you have a pool be sure to supply some plastic cups and plates for use around the pool.

Consider the needs of any young families who may want to rent your property. You should offer a cot and highchair at the very least. You may also need security stair gates which can be fitted during changeover. Plus bedding for the cot, a changing mat and baby monitor.

You should leave toilet rolls in the bathroom, along with some miniature sized toiletries for your guests.

You will need some outside furniture too, even if you only have a balcony or small terrace. A patio table and some chairs is a must, a BBQ would be nice and if you have the space, some sun loungers. Think about the children again and maybe have some swings or a slide.

When you are furnishing and equipping your home try to think what you would like to be provided with if you were holidaying at this house. If you ever think that some thing in your holiday home is "adequate" replace it with something better.

Don't put anything in your property that would cause you concern if it got lost or damaged. Don't try to "store" anything in your holiday home, such as such as under a bed. Anything in a holiday home is, as far as your guests are concerned, replaceable and for their exclusive use.

Have a lockable cupboard somewhere in the property so that you can store your personal possessions, extra bed linen and cleaning supplies.

The best way of being sure that your holiday home is well equipped and furnished is to actually stay in it. Have a holiday in your own home, if you find the property comfortable and have all the equipment you need then your guests are likely to feel the same!

Of course there is always the investment opportunity. You may be able to justify the expense of installing a hot tub, because you can charge a higher weekly rental rate to re-coup the costs.

The Garden and Outside Spaces

You will have to establish a pretty garden in your holiday home, then you will have to maintain it, which is easier said than done. It doesn't take very long at all for a garden to look neglected and untidy.

Try to plan for low maintenance gardens based on the climate of your area. Spend some time looking around your neighbours' gardens to see what they are growing. Find out the type of soil you have then visit the local garden centre to discover which plants will grow well. Avoid plants which need lots of regular attention, like rose bushes.

Lay patios or terraces in local stone for outside spaces such as for dining, sun-bathing or reading. You can always place pots around the edges of the areas.With the right choice of plants they could be left out all year.

Avoid gravel and timber decking unless it is laid over concrete, in no time at all it will be full of weeds and you will regret ever doing it!

Annual flowering plants are too high maintenance and should be avoided. Herbs are a good choice and of course, you or your guests can use them in the kitchen.

You could consider employing a local gardener to come in on a regular basis to keep the weeds down, dead head the flowers and cut the grass.

Try to have some higher plants or trees around the dining area in the garden to give a bit of privacy. If you can't wait for things to grow that tall consider putting up some trellis. Later you could place some climbing plants around it.

If you have a pool or are thinking of installing one, don't plant trees nearby, the leaves will only find their way into the pool making it difficult and time consuming to clean. Check the local laws on pool safety, in some areas in ground pools have to be securely fenced off to ensure young children don't fall in accidentally.

Make sure your garden is enclosed and secure, especially if you are likely to have families with young children visiting.

Don't forget to allow some space for parking a couple of cars outside your holiday home.

Taking Photographs

Before you start to advertise your holiday property you will have to take some photos, good photos. It's true "A picture tells a thousand words"! Your photos will have to show potential visitors why they should chose to rent your holiday home over others in your area. Your photos must show a property which is prettier, brighter and more inviting than your competitors.

If you can afford a professional photographer great! It will be worth the investment. However most people can produce a great representation of their property with a little forethought and planning.

Chose a bright, sunny day so that the rooms look warm. Take the photos when the sun is highest. You should put ceiling lights so long as you don't show them in the photos. Photos of bedrooms with bedside lamps switched on can give the impression that the room must be naturally dark.

Lay the table with pretty crockery and glasses, put a vase of flowers on the table and perhaps a bottle of wine. Plump up the cushions on the sofas and the pillows on the beds. The bedding must have been ironed. Make sure the curtains are tied back nicely.

If you have a fireplace you could light a fire or place some candles in the hearth.

Make it all look inviting!

Take time in dressing the property, this is going to be your "window" to the world so make it really special. Take several photos of every room, from different angles, and from different heights if possible. Take some photos with and without using the flash on your camera.

Make use of mirrors, try to be creative, perhaps taking a photo of a room through a mirror. Or if you have mirrored wardrobes take the photo towards the mirrors so that the room is reflected making it look bigger.

Take photos of any special features you might have such as a four poster bed, or a games room.

Apply the same thought to the outside of your property. Put window boxes full of flowers on the windowsills, or a flowerpot near the front door. Perhaps you could put a pretty bench outside or find an old bicycle to prop up against the wall.

If you have an outdoor eating area, dress the table by putting out some wine glasses and a basket of flowers or a bowl of fruit on the table, put up the parasol. If you have sun loungers drape a beach towel over one and maybe leave a book on another. Make sure the garden is tidy and the grass recently cut. If you have a pool try to photograph that from above looking down into the bright, clear, blue water.

If you have a good view take photos of that too, perhaps from an upstairs window.

Be critical of your photos. Go through them all checking for flaws such as:

- TV or lamp cables trailing
- a pet in the garden
- your reflection in a mirror
- an obstruction outside a window

If you're not happy with any of your photos, go back and take more and check them again until you are sure you have the best possible description of your holiday home.

Once you are sure everything is looking wonderful and you are pleased with your photos why not take a video film of your property? Walk slowly round your property whilst filming. Start with the garden then move indoors and move from room to room as if you were taking a visitor on a guided tour.

It's very easy to upload and edit your video on www.youtube.com you can even add background music and text credits to your film. This is a great advertising advantage.

Once you have all the photos and film of your beautiful holiday home you might consider taking some photos of the local area. Anything which may be of interest to your potential visitors. There may be a great beach nearby, or a chateau, or an aqua park. Visit your local tourist office to get ideas.

Marketing Your Property

Today, only about 20% of people go to a Travel Agent to book their holiday. As many as 60% use the internet to book an entire holiday, including travel arrangements. So most of your advertising should be internet based.

You might want to start by thinking of a name for your property. Consider the location and whether you are advertising a luxury apartment or a country cottage. Something like "Belle Vue" might suit a beachside property, but try to refrain from something like "Rose Cottage" unless your cottage is indeed in rural England and is positively bristling with roses.

Think about the sound of the name you chose. I hear all the time from our guests that they decided to look at our website just because they liked the name.

A this stage you should think about logos, colours and the shape of any text you might want to use on any advertising materials. Or indeed any colours you don't want! In general terms, dark colours for the background does not work well on the internet. Nor does yellow text!

There are lots of websites which have easy, step-by-step instructions on how to build your own website. They supply pre-designed templates in different styles and colours, you just have to add your text and upload your photos. Look at www.1and1.co.uk or www.ipage.com for ideas and more information. This is often a good option if you don't have a huge budget for marketing.

If you don't have the skills and knowledge required to create, upload to the internet and maintain your own website, it's well worth employing a talented web designer to do this for you. Of course, a recommendation is always the best route to take, if that's not possible, there are lots of good designers out there who will be more than happy to build to your specifications. You can always ask to look at some sites they have built previously.

Look around the internet, find sites you like the look and feel of. There will often be a link at the bottom of the page to the designer's own website.

Most designers offer a package deal of a few hundred pounds, money well spent for something that will last for years and years and be available 24 hours a day 365 days a year.

Your website should be designed so that it is easy to navigate from one page to another, and your contact email address and phone numbers should be clearly displayed.

Your website will be the window to your holiday home, it must look inviting and give a professional impression. Use the photos we talked about in the previous chapter and either include the video of have a link to it. Add captions to your photos so that visitors to the website know what they are looking at.

Give lots of information about your property, including any "wow" factors that you may be lucky enough to have. But be honest, don't exaggerate or you will end up with complaints. Try to come up with a "headline" which describes the best features of your property which will attract the attention of potential guests. Something like "Beautiful Country Cottage with Pool", or maybe "Luxury Apartment Overlooking Beach".

Check your grammar and spelling thoroughly.

I'm not a fan of having an availability page showing which weeks are booked and which are still available. This page of your website would need to be updated on a regular basis indicating any weeks booked. If you're not very technical it could become complicated. However, my own pet reason for not having such a page is that I want people to contact me directly. OK, maybe the week they wanted is booked, but I can sometimes offer them the week before or the week after. And they often take the alternative week.

Once your website is built and launched there are very low maintenance overheads involved in keeping it up and running all day every day, so it is a very cost effective way of marketing.

A nice touch is to have a downloadable colour brochure directly from your website.

There are holiday home agency websites who list lots of available holiday homes all over the world. They usually have an "advertise with us" button, where you will find details of how to add information and photos of your property. Some sites are free forever to the owner to advertise their holiday home. These sites seem to generate their income from links to other travel sites.

You will also find holiday rental agency websites who make an annual charge for advertising. However lots of these offer a 6 or even 12 months free trial. If, after the trial period you have been overwhelmed by bookings then you can think about forking out some cash to pay to be included in that site for the following 12 months.

On the other hand if you've had no enquiries that panned out from a particular site during the free trial period there seems little point in paying to continue to advertise with that company. Again, beware, it is not unknown for the owners of such sites to send bogus enquiries to unsuspecting property owners. Then when the owners are approached to pay for subsequent advertising the agency can claim that they have in fact generated enquiries. The fact that no one actually booked through this site apparently being neither here nor there.

Once you have chosen where to advertise your property you should be able to cut and paste everything from your own website onto theirs. Make sure you use your headline to give the greatest impact to your advertisement. You will also be able to upload all your beautiful photos and don't forget the captions!

We advertise on lots of free holiday rental sites and pay on only two good sites which have produced lots of bookings for us over the years.

It's worth spending a couple of days scouring the internet for companies who offer free trials for advertising your holiday home.

If you have your own website it's worth looking for other sites which allow you to add your URL, this is the address of your website. This is a good step towards moving your site up the search engine listings. The more links you have to your site the better.

Be inventive when searching for sites where you can add your URL and try specialist sites. For instance if there's good fishing nearby try looking for sites which are all about fishing holidays. Or maybe sites especially for family holidays if that's what you're offering.

The local Tourist Office website may well have a section for accommodation where you can add a few descriptive lines of your holiday home and maybe even a photo.

Some Ferry companies and Travel Agencies offer full package holidays to their clients and produce a shiny colour brochure with details of lots of holiday homes. For you, this does take all the worry out of advertising and finding guests. They advertise your holiday home and take bookings on your behalf. They also deal with payments from the guests and will send you a bulk payment, if applicable, along with details of any bookings, every month. All you have to think about is making sure your property is ready to receive the guests when they arrive. Of course, these companies charge a commission which can be as high as 30%, a sizeable chunk of your profit.

We did try this for one season in the early days, but we found that we could get more bookings via our web site. I felt this system lacked the personal touch too. For instance, for enquiries that come through our web site, by the time two or three emails have been exchanged, we usually know that the second week in July is booked to Mum & Dad and two children, a boy of 10 and a girl of 14 who live near Nottingham. All we got from the agency was a name and the number in the party. If fact they were sadly lacking in information as to the expected arrival times of guests.

You may chose to advertise in national newspapers, especially if they are planning a Pull-Out Holiday Special, but usually this can be quite expensive. A cheaper option is a periodical which specialises in small ads. Some specialist newspapers even allow free classified advertising.

You should also design business cards and a brochure in the same style as your website; with the same headline, logo, colours, fonts and at least one photo on your business card, but more in the brochure, so that everything is co-ordinated.

You can order some good quality business cards online at www.cardsmadeeasy.com by uploading photos and text from your website. Always carry them and give them out to anyone you meet. Leave a few in your holiday home, your guests will probably take them home. In which case they will have the information to hand if they want to book again next year or they might pass your card on to friends who are interested.

Design a brochure with as much information as possible taken from your website. Add photos, rental rates and contact email addresses and phone numbers.

Put your brochure on the notice board at work, the local supermarket, or in the library, maybe even your hairdresser will allow you a small display. Look around your town to find possible places where you could benefit from some free advertising. Talk to local bar owners and restaurateurs, ask if you can leave your brochures on the bar. Make sure the local Tourist Office has a constant supply. Keep everything updated and make sure all your outlets are well supplied.

It may be that you already have a free email account with hotmail or yahoo. This is fine for personal use, but when used for a business they just smack of cheapness. Lets say your holiday home is called Shangrila, if you use hotmail for your email, your address might be shangrila@hotmail.com. But once you have a website you will have with it several personalised email address. You will be able to customise these addresses such as:

- info@shangrila.com

- sales@shangrila.com

- mary@shangrila.com

These look much more professional. Don't forget you are asking people who have never met you, to part with their money, they must feel confident that they are dealing with a bona fida business.

Marketing does not stop once your guests book. Most property owners take a deposit at the time of booking, the balance being due a few weeks prior to arrival. So, when you send the confirmation of booking, why not include a sticky label which has your name and logo and the words "It's only 6 weeks to our holiday". Suggest that your prospective guests stick it on their calendar. For them it's a reminder, for you it's advertising to anyone who happens to spot their calendar.

It doesn't stop after your guests leave either. Design a Welcome Home card and have several in stock at any given time. Post one off a few days prior to the departure of your guests so that it's on the door mat for them by the time they get home. It will remind them of their wonderful holiday!

Then there's Christmas, you could send cards to the people who have stayed with you during that year and, as times go on, a few special people who have been guests with you on previous years.

Keep a Vistors' Book in your holiday home. Not everyone will write in your book, those who do are likely to be complimentary about their holiday "home from home", and they may add information for subsequent guests, such as recommending a restaurant or a local town to visit.

Take these comments and add them to a "Guest Book" page on your website, always having asked permission to do so first. Email your visitors after their stay and ask if they will write a review on www.Tripadvisor.co.uk for you. Most travellers will visit Tripadvisor prior to booking any aspect of their holiday.

Setting Rental Rates

The rental rate you can expect to receive for your holiday home will be based upon several criteria;

- The standard of your property, i.e. furnishings, decoration and cleanliness

- The location

- The number of bedrooms and bathrooms

- Facilities inside the property such as en-suite bathrooms, fitted kitchen, comfy sofas, TV, DVD players, washing machine etc.

- Facilities outside the property such as parking, patio, BBQ, garden, garden furniture, pool, hot tub etc.

- Optional extras, which other proprietors may charge for, such as towels and bed linen.

You will also have to consider the rental rates of other local properties, the opposition. So that may well be a very good place to start.

A visit to the local tourist office should supply you with lots of information on property available for rent in your area.

In fact that might be quite an education, you may well be surprised, or disappointed at what your competition is charging.

If you are very brave, you may even chance giving one of your competitors a call and arranging a viewing pretending to be a prospective guest. However, bear in mind that such a visit could send you into a panic, and have you replacing all your interior moderate furniture with something a lot more exclusive, and therefore a lot more expensive!

You must use some common sense when working out rental rates, it's no good trying to justify unrealistically high prices just because you want to earn a certain figure per year. You will end up pricing yourself out of the market. But if you have a beautiful holiday home with every possible luxury available then you will be in a position to charge accordingly.

You could look online on holiday rental websites for similar properties in your area to see what everyone else is charging.

You will have to work out different rates for different times of the year. Obviously you will be able to charge more in summer months than in the winter, the highest rate being during school holidays.

If there are occasions during the year near your property, such as music festivals or sports events, you will be able to charge more for rentals during those times.

Decide on a minimum stay, which again could vary depending on the time of year. You might be happy to rent you property out for a long week-end in October but stick to 7 nights minimum in the summer.

If you are considering offering short breaks, remember the costs of changeover and laundry. You may find that rental costs for 3 or 4 nights only just cover the expenses.

Depending on where you are advertising you may need to indicate your rates in different currencies.

You should also make it very clear what, exactly, is included in your rates and what is not, for instance

- gas
- electricity
- water
- bed linen
- accommodating pets

You can always offer "Special Offers" or "Late Escapes" if you have odd weeks available in the short term. Offering a discount of 20% is better than having an empty property.

Be specific about different rates, "Low Season" may not mean much to your potential guests, but "January 1st to March 31st" is much clearer.

You should also state how much security deposit you will require, make it clear how you expect the property to be left and under what circumstances you will make a charge.

Administration

If you have been the sort of person who checks their email once a week then that is all about to change!

Prompt and professional response to any enquiry is paramount. There are lots of holiday homes out there and the chances are that your enquirer has emailed more than one about availability for their holiday. They won't wait more than 48 hours for a response. Aim to answer any enquiry as soon as is possible.

As you now have your own website, you will have several email address you can customise. At the very least you should have 2 email addresses which you can easily set up via the Control Panel of your website.

Let's concentrate on the first one for now, it might be something like *info@willow-cottage.com*. There should be an easy to find button on your website which says "Click here to email about availability" which directs any enquiries to this email address. If you advertise on holiday home rental sites make sure you use the same email address on there too.

The immediate enquiry, lets say it's some one asking if the first week in August is available and for confirmation of the price, will always go to the first email address; *info@willow-cottage.com*

Set this email account to generate an autoresponse; an instant response to the enquirer. Again you can customise the text within the response, I have included a sample in Chapter 14. At the very least your enquirer knows that you have received their email message, but they will be impressed at such a quick reply.

Once you see the email message on your computer you answer it via a different email address, such as sally*@willow-cottage.com* - much more personal yet professional too.

I suggest that you keep a draft copy of few relevant basic email responses, saves time typing the same thing over and over again.

So your response might be some thing along the lines of:

Hello (type in the enquirer's name here)

Thank you for your enquiry. Yes, the cottage is available for the first week in August. The price for that week would be £xxx which includes all bed linen and towels.

Looking forward to hearing from you.

Kind regards

Your name

Your telephone number

Your email address

Your website address

Your enquirer, having received an email from *sally@willow-cottage.com* will simply click on "reply" so any responses they chose to send will go back to *sally@willow-cottage.com* rather than *info@willow-cottage.com*

Using 2 email address as described above means that you can use the autoresponder option. If you only had one address and used the autoresponder, everytime some one emailed you at that address they would get the automatically generated response and we don't need or want to do that.

This might be a good place to talk about the format of your email messages. If this is beyond your technical talents get some one to do it all for you, it should only take about half an hour or so. Arrange your email so that messages are written in a font and colour that is similar to your website. Create a signature to automatically add to your messages, so that you don't need to type it in every time. Your signature should include your name, address, phone numbers, email address and website address.

Once you have established that your property is available for the specified dates required and the enquirer wants to make a firm booking you will need a good system. This must ensure that the enquirer, who has now become the potential guest, knows how much deposit you want, how to pay it, when the balance will be due, how much security deposit you require, and you should also make your guests aware of your Terms and Conditions.

You will need a good calendar with space to write down which weeks are booked, who has paid deposits and who have made balance payments. The last thing you want is a double booked week!!!

Suggest that your guests pay 25% deposit at the time of booking, some proprietors hold this as a security deposit, others expect cash on arrival. The balance of the rental costs normally can be paid six weeks before they arrive for their holiday.

Offer a variety of payment methods; UK cheque, direct on-line transfer into your bank account, or by bank or credit card via PayPal. However, Paypal add on about 3.5% for charges so you must include this cost when advising your guests.

Your documents should all reflect the style and fonts on your website. Headed paper should be in "your" colours, have your logo, the property name, your website address and email address. Everything should be uniform.

Once you receive the deposit send a confirmation either by post or as an attachment via email. Include local driving directions and a copy of your guest itinerary. There is no point in your guests bringing something from home which you already supply, plus they will appreciate knowing what is available for their use.

Your Terms and Conditions should be clearly printed on your confirmation documents. This should include the booking requirements, arrival and departure times, what the price includes and what it does not. What should happen if the holiday is cancelled either by your guests or by yourself. Travel Insurance information and any disclaimers you want to include.

You must decide on your cancellation policy. You may want come up with a sliding scale of funds returned, such as 50% of the balance returned if they cancel within 5 weeks of arrival, but only 20% if they cancel within 2 weeks of arrival.

Even after you have secured a booking keep an eye on your email, your prospective guests might need to ask questions about local restaurants or supermarket opening times.

Once you receive the balance payment you should email your guests and let them know. After all, these people have sent a chunk of their hard-earned money to someone they have never met, so they need to be sure their money is where it should be!

At this point it is a good idea to establish what time your guests will arrive. Ask that people vacate by a certain time, say 10.00am and tell them that they cannot gain access until at lease 1.pm which gives you a minimum of 3 hours for changeover, which is a whole new subject!

You will find sample documents at the end of this book.

Changeover

Saturday is the traditional day for changeovers, the day when one family moves out and, hopefully, when another moves in. This is fine if you have only one property and live on site. If you have more than one property, but still live on site remember that even the fastest cleaner will have a job getting two holiday homes ready for new guests in just a few hours.

If you don't live on site and are depending on asking a neighbour to act as key holder, (I can't imagine a more random description) bear in mind that there are only so many hours in the day.

Of course, alternative days should always be considered. After all, travelling mid week can often be cheaper, so this will not necessarily have a negative impact upon holiday bookings, it may in fact be more beneficial.

Ask your guests to leave about 10.am. Occasionally some families will leave very early, in which case, check out can be conducted the evening before. Although there will be other guests who's flight or ferry doesn't leave until 6pm, so they will be in no hurry to leave and might sit on the patio until the last possible minute before you will have to go and eject them!

Make it clear if you offer a Cleaning Service at the end of your guests' stay, or if they are expected to clean up before they leave.

Check the property for any damage, but always ask your departing visitors if there has been any accidents, as you may not notice until you are cleaning that, for instance, the loo seat is broken. Most people will admit to breaking a wine glass and most proprietors would not charge for a replacement. However, there will be times when your guests will have an accident or cause damage and won't tell you.

I deal with this by thinking that it's their conscience, and accepting that these people have no respect for anyone else's property. Damage is something which, sadly, must be expected, whether admitted to or not.

Security deposits can be returned at this time minus any damage you have found, or that your guests have mentioned.

It may be prudent to make a separate charge for electricity based on the units used. The electricity meter would be read and charges paid at check out time.

You may decide to offer optional extras, such as a baby sitting service, or the supply of logs for the woodburner during the colder months.

If you find something left behind by accident you can email your guests to ask if they want it returned by post but make it clear that it will be at their expense.

Your property must be cleaned to the highest standard on the departure of every guest. Cleaning a holiday home is not the same as cleaning your own home. If you have furnished and equipped your holiday home properly, there will be a place for everything. It's not a dynamic property, there won't be new photos in picture frames suddenly appearing. Notes won't be pinned on the fridge nor will clutter have built up.

But your new guests who are just arriving should find no trace of those who have just departed.

If you found some crumbs in your cutlery drawer you would probably think "Oh I'll clean that up later", it's your crumbs in your drawer. But if your guests arrive, weary from their journey and just want a cup of tea, but open the cutlery drawer to find some else's crumbs - that's a whole different scenario!

Your property should be verging on clinical as far as cleanliness goes. It's the one paramount aspect that all your guests will expect.

Beds should be made up ready for the new guests. Hand and bath towels, kitchen and tea towels should be supplied along with fresh bath mats. Leave supplies of soap, kitchen paper towels, toilet rolls and toiletries.

Leave a folder in the property with all the information you think your guests might need;

- how to operate the TV and home entertainment systems
- how to operate all the kitchen appliances
- how to access to the internet
- information on the mains services available
- where the dustbins are located
- local restaurants

- tourist information

- list of emergency contact numbers

You will find that you will have to state the obvious. I used to include a sentence asking guests to strip the beds prior to their departure, until I found that some one stripped all 4 beds despite only using one.

If you are expecting your visitors to clean up before they go, ensure there are plenty of cleaning materials and cloths available in the kitchen and bathroom.

Consider leaving a supply of tea, coffee, sugar, milk, bottled water and some local wine for each family. A vase of fresh flowers on the dining room table are a good idea too.

Minor maintenance on the properties, such as replacing light bulbs, can be carried out where possible during changeovers. Check that everything is working and that the remote controls have functioning batteries. General wear and tear has to be anticipated too. Toilet brushes need replacing regularly and tea towels often have to be discarded after use.

The garden will have to be checked and the lawn mown if necessary. Don't forget to check if your departing guests cleaned the BBQ.

Ask your potential guests to indicate their expected arrival time. It may be best to suggest an arrival window of a couple of hours in the afternoon when you have had time to complete the cleaning and preparation.

If you live on site, try to be on hand to welcome your new guests and show them around the property. Have a contingency plan in case your guests can't find your property. We always ask any lost guests to drive to the next village and park in front of the church, easily found due to the spire. Then I go find them and bring them back to Hirondelle Farm.

A Check-in form is a good idea to use for noting the electricity meter reading and for adding the cost of optional extras.

Make sure your guests know where you live and how to get hold of you if there is a problem, then wish them a Happy Holiday!

Keep a list of contact numbers for local plumbers, electricians e.t.c. for an emergency out of your scope of expertise.

Property Management

We are fortunate, in that we live on the same site as our holiday homes. Most people are not lucky enough to enjoy that pleasure. In which case someone else will have to be employed to clean your property and prepare it for new guests.

Some people offer what they refer to as a "key holding" service. I can't imagine a broader phrase.

Guests who will be paying to rent your a holiday home will expect a spotlessly clean, well equipped property. They will want comfortable beds, good furniture, pretty decor, attention to detail and as I said in Chapter 9 no trace of the previous visitors.

A "key holder" will not expect to do much more than see one family out, perhaps change the beds and be available to hand over the key to the next lot of visitors. If that is what you want then that's fine, but don't expect anyone to re-book for next year or write a good review for you on Tripadvisor. It all depends on what you expect to get out of your holiday home. You will get out what you put in.

My Property Management Company was approached once by a new holiday home owner asking for a quote to deal with changeover in her property. I gave her a full account of our services and costs, but she said "Oh! I won't need all of that, I shall ask everyone to leave it clean when they go". She came back to me after her first season; she had so many complaints about the cleanliness and general state of the property.

Your standards should be very high, they need to be. Gone are the days when holidaymakers accept a property which has only basic amenities and looks like it hasn't seen a duster for months.

A good Property Management Company will work very hard in a professional manner doing everything that you would do if you were present. They will ensure that the property and gardens are pristine, that all the laundry is organised. They will welcome your guests, show them around, read meters and give them contact details should any problems arise.

They should also be familiar with the area so that they can recommend places to visit and things to do locally.

They will see your guests out at the end of their holiday, check the property, deal with returning security deposits and start all over again for your next lot of guests.

They will deal with the garden, cleaning the pool if you have one, cutting the lawns and general maintenance of the property.

Of course there will be costs for using a Property Management Company, allow for about a third of your rental income. But it's a small price to pay for peace of mind and the confidence in knowing that your property is safe and that your guests are happy.

Dealing With Complaints

Good communication with your guests is vital in avoiding complaints in the first place. Make sure your confirmation letter and Terms and Conditions explain any rules you have, such as no smoking in the property.

Be honest in your advertising, don't say you have a 32" TV screen if you only have a 27" TV.

If you know something is broken, take it out and replace it as soon as you possible can. If you can't replace it immediately tell your arriving guests and explain what you are planning to do about it.

Unfortunately there may come a time when you will have to deal with a complaint. If you have a Property

Management Company they will have experience of handling these situations. Nonetheless, you should agree with your Management Company the rate of recompense. You wouldn't want them handing back a full week's rental as a refund for a petty problem.

But if you have to sort out the problem your self then do it quickly and without fuss. If it's a small problem such as the coffee machine breaking down, replace it as soon as possible, that same day if you can. You might also like to offer a bottle of local wine as compensation.

If it's a more serious problem, such as the hot water system failing and your guests being unable to shower that morning, but the plumber is on his way, then you will need to give some sort of refund, perhaps one nights' rental.

On the other hand if your plumber says he can't come out to fix it until the end of the week, you will have to find alternative accommodation for your guests. You may also have to give a refund of a couple of nights rental to compensate for the hassle of moving to another property.

Whatever the problem, keep calm, try to be sympathetic to your guests and fix it fast. Of course if you get more than one complaint about the same thing then it is something that must be investigated thoroughly.

The Law

You should take advice from an accountant, financial advisor, or tax expert as to your how much, if any, tax you will have to pay on the income you generate from your holiday home. You may have to pay tax in the country where you live and in the country where your property is based. Tax laws vary so much that going into detail here is beyond the scope of this book.

You should speak to a lawyer who is familiar with the legislation in the country where your holiday home is situated. There may be local laws about short term letting.

You may need to register the property as a business. Visit your local Town Hall to check that you comply with any bylaws.

You will need insurance for the property itself and public liability insurance in case one of your guests is somehow injured whilst staying at your property.

Check the fire safety regulations to make sure you property complies. Have all the electric and gas equipment checked that they are all safe and working correctly.

Sample Documents

I have gathered a collection of the documents I use in taking bookings, sending confirmations, plus my terms and Conditions.

Auto-Response

(This is my automatic response to an enquiry received by email)

Hello

Thank you for your enquiry.

I am not at my PC at the moment, but I will respond very soon! In the meantime if you have found Hirondelle Farm through a Holiday Agency Site you may want to visit our own web site where you will find more information: www.hirondelle-farm.com

Plus we have a short video on You Tube here:

http://www.youtube.com/watch?v=B8ZppkruYa4

Or, if you have any questions you may want to look at our FAQ (Frequently Asked Questions) page on our web site. If your enquiry is urgent you may want to send me a text message on: 00 33 679 37 33 77

Kind regards,

Dori Joyner

Hirondelle Farm

Formal First Response

(Your response to an enquiry, insert numbers and dates as necessary)

Hello (insert name)

Thank you for your enquiry.

Yes, the Stable is available, at the moment, for? weeks from Saturday? 2013 to Saturday? 2013. The price includes all bed linen, hand and bath towels, kitchen and tea towels, gas, water, exclusive use of the pool and Wi-Fi.

Please note we can also offer you 20% discount on Brittany Ferry crossings.

Looking forward to hearing from you.

Kind regards,

Dori Joyner

Hirondelle Farm

Accepting a Booking

Hello (insert name)

We are delighted to accept your booking for the Stable for? weeks from Saturday? 2013 to Saturday?2013.

We normally ask for a 25% deposit at the time of booking, in this case £?. UK cheque is fine, made payable to "D Joyner" and sent to the address below. Don't forget the European stamp or you will be here before the cheque!

Or if you use internet banking you can do an on-line transfer to:

Lloyds TSB

Sort Code: 12 34 56

Acc No: 012345678

Name: Mrs DE Joyner

Or I can send you a link to pay by PayPal or bank/credit card.However,PayPal add on 3.5% for PayPal, bank or credit card transactions to cover their charges. So please let me know which method you prefer.

When I receive your cheque, or on-line transfer, or funds via PayPal or bank/credit card, I will email you to advise of its safe arrival and I will include a confirmation along with driving directions etc.

The balance of £? can be paid either 6 weeks prior to arrival, which would be? 2013. Again, when I receive your balance cheque, or on-line transfer, or funds via PayPal or bank/credit card, I will email you to advise of it's safe arrival.

Looking forward to hearing from you.

Kind regards,

Dori Joyner

Hirondelle Farm

Confirmation Letter

Dear Sally and Ian

Thank you for your booking and deposit of £85.

We can confirm that the Stable has been reserved for your holiday for the following dates:

Saturday 7th September 2013 to Saturday 14th September 2013

The balance of £255 will be payable by 30th July 2013.

Please note that the price includes all linen, gas for cooking and water for basic domestic use. Electricity will be charged at the rate of €0.20 per unit, we provide UK electrical points, no need to bring an adaptor. A €200/ £150 cash deposit is payable on arrival to cover any damage. This will be returned on departure minus any necessary deductions.

You are asked to arrive at the property not before 1.00 pm on your arrival date and to please vacate the property by 10.00 am on your departure morning. Once you have booked your crossing please let us know your estimated time of arrival so that we can be here to welcome you.

We always provide a welcome pack of tea, coffee, sugar, milk and a bottle of wine for our guests. However, if you plan to arrive late on Saturday please remember that the supermarkets are closed on Sundays, so either shop en-route or bring enough food with you to sustain your group until Monday.

I have enclosed some local directions to help you plan the trip, but you can find us on Google Earth and Google Maps.

Yours sincerely,

Dori Joyner

Inventory

This is a list of what we provide in the Stable, I send it with the confirmation:

Kitchen

- Electric Fan Oven
- Gas Hob
- Fridge
- Dishwasher and tablets
- Microwave
- Toaster
- Electric kettle
- Coffee machine and filters
- Crockery and cutlery
- Saucepans, frying pan and as-near-to-a-wok-as-I-can-find-in-France
- Tea pot
- Selection of glasses and tumblers
- Towels and tea towels
- Iron and board

- Kitchen roll

- Soap

- Broom

- Dustpan and brush

- Mop and bucket

- Vacuum Cleaner

Lounge

- Satellite TV

- DVD Player

- Radio and CD player

- Pool table

- Board games

- Books

- Reading lamps

Bedrooms

- All bed Linen

- Pillows

- Clothes hangers

- Bedside lamps

- Mirrors

- Tissues

- Selection of books

Bathroom
- Hand and bath towels

- Bath mat

- Shaving mirror

- Toilet rolls

- Personal Toiletries

Landing Cupboards
- Spare blankets

- Extra pillows

- mobile oscillating fan

Outside
- Pool

- Patio furniture and parasol

- BBQ

- Garden lights

- Sun loungers

- Lawned garden

- Washing line and pegs

Extras
- Cot

- High chair

- Changing mat

- Baby bath

- Baby monitor

- Stair gates

Just for you..............
- Free Wi-Fi

- Tea

- Coffee

- Sugar

- Milk

- Condiments and herbs

- Bottle of local wine

Example Terms and Conditions

Booking

A non-refundable deposit 25% of the total rental price is required on booking, the balance is due no later than 6 weeks prior to the beginning of the letting period. A binding contract exists when we receive your deposit payment. The persons on your party should not differ under any circumstances to the persons stated at the time of enquiry. Unless otherwise stated bookings are for a minimum of 1 week and run from Saturday to Saturday in the Stable, and Sunday to Sunday in the FarmHouse. For bookings made less than 6 weeks prior the beginning of the letting period, the payment must be made in full.

Arrival/Departure

You are asked to arrive at the property not before 1.00 pm on your arrival date and to please vacate the property by 10.00 am on your departure morning. Please advise us of your expected arrival time.

What the Price Includes

The price of your holiday accommodation is charged at a weekly rate and includes all bed linen, hand and bath towels, kitchen and tea towels, gas for cooking and water for basic domestic use. A stock of logs for the woodburner is provided for our guests' arrival during the winter months.

What the Price Does Not Include

Electricity will be charged at the rate of €0.20 per unit. Extra logs for the woodburner can be supplied at a cost of €5 per load. A €200 or £150 cash deposit is payable on arrival to cover any damage. This will be returned on departure minus any necessary deductions. You agree to identify and compensate us for any damage caused by you or yours.

Alterations to your Booking by You

It is our policy to make alterations to your booking free of charge. However, in the case where additional costs may incur, these should be paid in full by you.

Cancellation of your Booking by You

If you cancel your booking you will immediately lose any deposit payments due to us, unless we agree to do otherwise. 50% of the total price is due if you cancel between 60 and 30 days prior to the beginning of the letting period. The full amount is due when cancellations are made 30 days prior to the beginning of the letting period.

Travel Insurance

Although Travel Insurance is not compulsory, we do strongly advise you to take out a policy. Always check the small print of a travel insurance policy to ensure it meets your individual requirements. No liability under any circumstances will be accepted by us for a damage to luggage, motor vehicles and personal effects owned by you. Our Responsibility

We cannot be held liable or accept responsibility in any circumstances for your illness, bodily harm, death or discomfort. Neither can we be held liable or accept responsibility in any circumstances for your illness, bodily harm, death or discomfort as a result of suggestions made in any of our information.

If we alter your Holiday in any Way

No compensation is payable where unforeseeable circumstances cause us to cancel your holiday either before your departure or during your holiday. Unforeseeable circumstances include: war - threat of war - civil strife - terrorist activity - industrial dispute - natural disaster, fire - sickness - accident - bad weather conditions and the results of these including water drought or shortage - the acts of any Government or public authority and all events of a similar nature beyond our control.

We reserve the right to curtail any rental agreement, immediately and without notice or refund, if, in our opinion, the property and/or any content is misused or abused.

Example Check in Form

Guests understand that the price includes all linen, gas for cooking and water for basic domestic use. Electricity will be charged at the rate of €0.20 per unit. Extra logs for the woodburner are available at a cost of €5 a basket. A €200/£150 cash deposit is payable on arrival to cover any damage. This will be returned at checkout on departure minus any necessary deductions.

Name...

Date of Arrival..

Deposit Received..

Elec meter reading on departure....................

Elec meter reading on arrival........................

Total Unit used..

Damage, if any..

Plus logs, if any..

TOTAL TO PAY...

13911273R00048

Printed in Poland
by Amazon Fulfillment
Poland Sp. z o.o., Wrocław